A Nice, Big Batch

By Sally Cowan

I love to learn new things!

Today Mum is teaching me how to bake.

I am going to make a batch of cupcakes in the kitchen.

I crack a large egg on the edge of the dish.

Mum helps me stir the mix
until I get the gist.

We put our hands on the bowl
to brace it.

When everything is mixed well,
I place the mix in thin cases.

Then we bake the batch of cupcakes!

They smell so good while they cook.

For the next stage,
we ice the cupcakes.

They look very nice!

Todd and his mum make a batch of fudge!

Todd's mum stirs the fudge mix in a pan on the stove.

Mum tips the fudge mix into a dish.

Todd makes space in the fridge and places the dish inside.

The fudge mix will chill until it's thick like cement!

When the fudge is set,
Todd fetches it from the fridge.

Mum can slice it into wedges
or cubes.

Todd would like cubes!

Clem and her dad make a batch of pumpkin-spice muffins with cinnamon.

They decide to change the method and add some sage.

Yum!

Which batch is the best?

You be the judge!

CHECKING FOR MEANING

1. Where did Todd place the fudge? *(Literal)*
2. What did Clem and her dad bake? *(Literal)*
3. Why do you need to brace the bowl with your hands while you mix the ingredients? *(Inferential)*
4. Has the author of this text convinced you to try making a batch of something? Why? *(Evaluative)*

EXTENDING VOCABULARY

batch	Read the word *batch*. How many sounds are in this word? What are the sounds? What batches did people make in the text?
wedges	What does a wedge look like? What foods are wedge-shaped?
spice	What are some different types of spice? Why do people add spices to food? What spices do you like? Are there any spices you don't like?

MOVING BEYOND THE TEXT

1. Each child made a batch of sweet treats. What other foods are baked in batches?
2. If you could bake something, what would you make? What ingredients might you use?
3. What are some rules to stay safe in the kitchen?
4. How can you learn to be a good baker?

TIME TO WRITE

Write about something you would like to make a batch of. Include what you might need and why you want to make it.